BREATH OF LIFE

Songbook

"Speak to one another with psalms, hymns and spiritual songs.
Sing and make music in your heart to the Lord,
Always giving thanks to God the Father for everything,
In the name of our Lord Jesus Christ"

Ephesians 5:19-20

Published by HTB Publications
Holy Trinity Brompton, Brompton Road, London SW7 1JA

Contents

ALL CREATION

Brian Doerksen & Steve Mitchinson

All pro - vi - sion, comes from__You.__ In ev-'ry__sun - rise, hope shines__through.__

For Your__mer - cy, we thank__You.__

All cre - a - tion looks to You.

All pro-vi - sion comes from You. {In ev-'ry rhy - thm we thank You, for Your__love.__
In ev-'ry sea - son we thank You, for your__love.__

5

LIFT UP YOUR HEADS, O YOU GATES

Graham Kendrick

WHO IS LIKE OUR GOD?

Brian Duane, Brian Doerksen & Brian Thiessen

TAKE MY LIFE AND LET IT BE

Words: Frances R Havergal (1874)
Music: David Clifton/Phil Baggaley

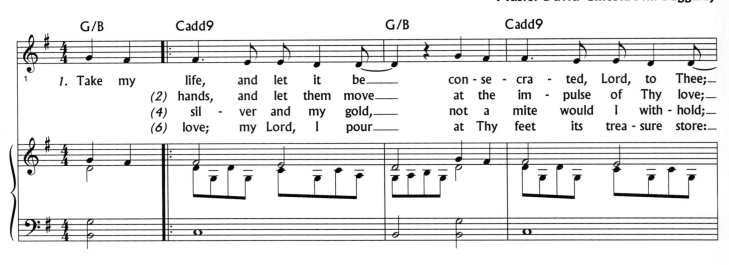

1. Take my life, and let it be consecrated, Lord, to Thee;
(2) hands, and let them move at the impulse of Thy love;
(4) silver and my gold, not a mite would I withhold;
(6) love; my Lord, I pour at Thy feet its treasure store:

take my moments and my days, let them flow in ceaseless praise.
take my feet, and let them be swift and beautiful for Thee.
take my intellect, and use Ev'ry pow'r as Thou shalt choose.
take myself, and I will be ever, only, all for Thee.

2. Take my

O BREATH OF LIFE

Words: Bessie Head (1850 - 1936)
Music: Andy Piercy

3. O Breath of love,⏜ come breathe with-in⏜ us,
4. Re - vive us, Lord,⏜ is zeal a - ba - ting

re - new - ing thought and will⏜ and heart.
while har - vest fields are vast⏜ and white?

Come, love of Christ,⏜ a - fresh⏜ to win us,
Re - vive us, Lord,⏜ the world⏜ is wait - ing,

re - vive⏜ Your church in ev - 'ry part.
e - quip⏜ Your church to spread⏜ the

light.

13

BE THE CENTRE

Michael Frye

1. Je - sus, be the cen - tre, be my source,

be my light, Je - sus.

MINE EYES HAVE SEEN THE GLORY

Julia W. Howe (1819-1910)

OPEN THE EYES OF MY HEART

Paul Baloche

SALVATION BELONGS TO OUR GOD

Adrian Turner and Pat Turner

ev - er_ and ev - er, be to our God for ev - er_ and ev - er, A -

1. men! 2. And men! men!

O LORD HEAR MY PRAYER

Jacques Berthier

IF I RISE

Jamie Haith

BREATHE

Marie Barnet

ALL CREATION

   A   D   E
We come to you with a heart of thanks for Your love

   A   D   A
To be a living sacrifice, brought with love

   A   D   E
We come to You with a heart of thanks for Your love

   A   D   A
An offering of all we are, brought with love

              D   E   A   D   A
All creation looks to You, all provision comes from You

                 D   E   A   D   A
In every sunrise, hope shines through; for Your mercy, we thank You

   A   D   E
We come to You with a song of praise for Your love

   A   D   A
The music of our soul's delight brought with love

   A   D   E
We come to You with a song of praise for Your love

A   D   A
Sounds of joy and gratefulness brought with love

                        D
All creation looks to You, all provision comes from You

   A   D   A
In every rhythm we thank You, for Your love.

                        D   A
[In every season we thank You, for Your love.]

CHORDS USED IN THIS SONG

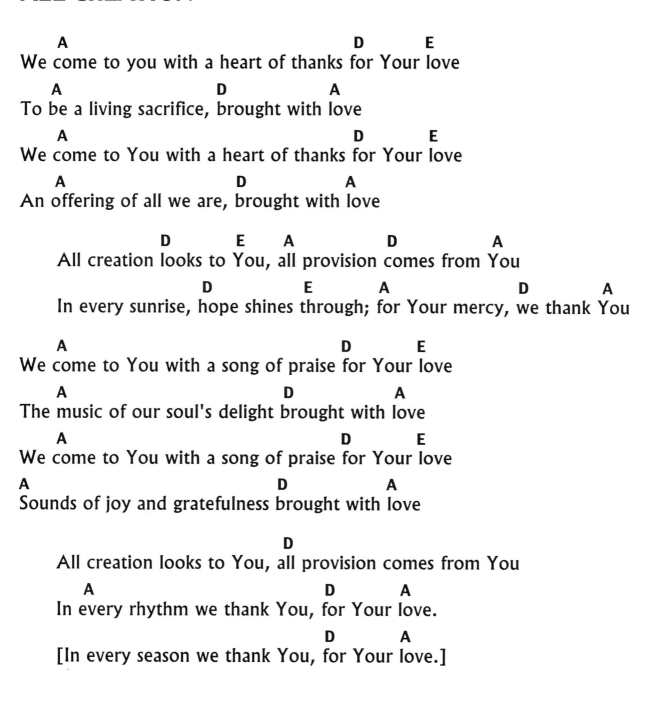

Brian Doerksen & Steve Mitchinson
Copyright © 1999 Vineyard Songs (UK/Eire)
37 Blagdon Road, New Malden, KT3 4AH, England.
Used by permission.

LIFT UP YOUR HEADS, O YOU GATES

```
          G       C    G                   D         G
Lift up your heads, O you gates, swing wide you everlasting doors
                    C    G                   D         G
Lift up your heads, O you gates, swing wide you everlasting doors

        G     C   D     Em      G    C    D        G
That the King of Glory may come in, that the King of Glory may come in
        G     C   D     Em      G    C    D
That the King of Glory may come in, that the King of Glory may come in

G C G D G C G D


        G    C   G                 D           G
Up from the dead He ascends, through every rank of heavenly power
              C    G                 D         G
Let heaven prepare the highest place, throw wide the everlasting doors


        G      C     G              D          G
With trumpet blast and shouts of joy, all heaven greets the risen King
              C    G
With angel choirs, come line the way,
          D                G
Throw wide the gates and welcome Him
```

CHORDS USED IN THIS SONG

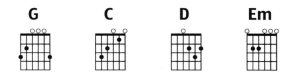

G   C   D   Em

Graham Kendrick
Copyright © 1991 Make Way Music
P.O. Box 263, Croydon, Surrey, CR9 5AP, UK.

WHO IS LIKE OUR GOD?

```
G       C2      G       C2      G       C2      G       C2
Who is like our God?        Who is like our God?
Em          Bm7     C           G       D/F♯
Holy and intimate, tender and strong,
Em          Bm7
Patient and powerful,
C       D       G   C2      G   C2
Who is like our God?


G       C2      G       C2  G   C2      G       C2
Who is like our God?        Who is like our God?
Em          Bm7     C           G       D/F♯
Mighty and innocent, jealous and kind,
Em          Bm7
Sovereign and merciful,
C       D       G   C2      G   C2
Who is like our God?


D               C
All of man's glory fades away
Em              D
Like a spring flower in the rain.
Am          Em      D/F♯                G
No fallen angel is worthy to be worshipped,
        F           D
Nor anything created.


G       C2      G       C2  G   C2      G       C2
Who is like our God?        Who is like our God?
```

CHORDS USED IN THIS SONG

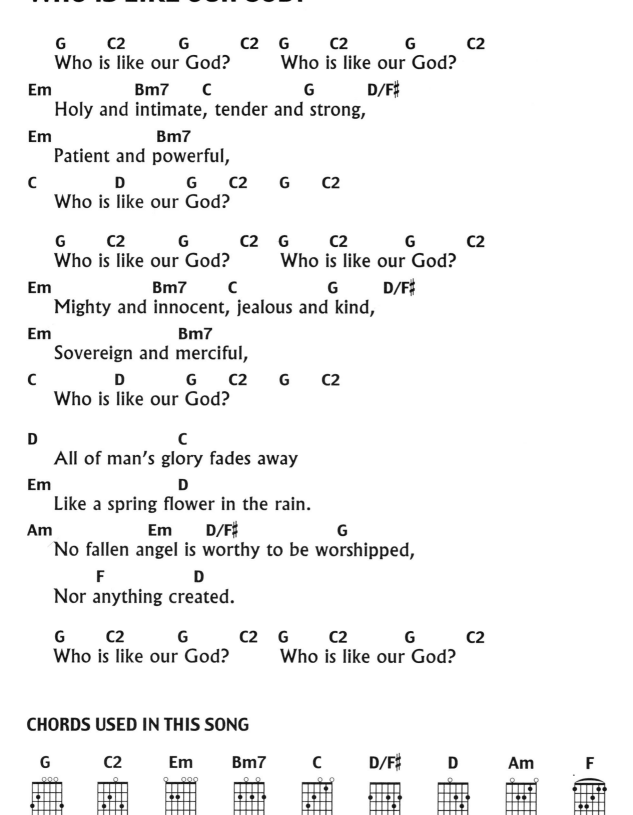

G   C2   Em   Bm7   C   D/F♯   D   Am   F

Brian Duane, Brian Doerksen & Brian Thiessen
Copyright © 1995 Vineyard Songs (UK/Eire)
37 Blagdon Road, New Malden, KT3 4AH, England.
Used by permission.

TAKE MY LIFE AND LET IT BE

     G/B   Cadd9   G/B   Cadd9   G/B

1.   Take my life and let it be consecrated Lord to Thee

          Cadd9   G/B   Am7   D7sus4 D7

    Take my moments and my days let them flow in ceaseless praise

     G/B   Cadd9   G/B   Cadd9   G/B

2.   Take my hands and let them move at the impulse of Thy love

          Cadd9   G/B   Am7   D7sus4 D7

    Take my feet and let them be swift and beautiful for Thee

      Am7   D7   G/B   Am7   D7 G/B

3.   Take my voice and let me sing always only for my King

      Am7   D7   G/B   Am7   D7sus4 D7

    Take my lips and let them be filled with messages from Thee

     G/B   Cadd9   G/B   Cadd9   G/B

4.   Take my silver and my gold not a mite would I withhold

          Cadd9   G/B   Am7   D7sus4 D7

    Take my intellect and use every power as Thou shalt choose

      Am7   D7   G/B   Am7   D7   G/B

5.   Take my will and make it Thine it shall be no longer mine

      Am7   D7   G/B   Am7   D7sus4 D7

    Take my heart it is Thine own it shall be Thy royal throne

     G/B   Cadd9   G/B   Cadd9   G/B

6.   Take my love my Lord I pour at Thy feet its treasure store

          Cadd9   G/B   Am7   D7sus4 D7 G (end)

    Take myself and I will be ever only all for Thee

CHORDS USED IN THIS SONG

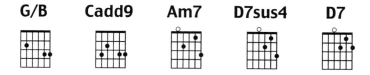

G/B   Cadd9   Am7   D7sus4   D7

Words: Frances R Havergal (1874)
Public Domain

Music: David Clifton/Phil Baggaley
Copyright © 1998 IQ Music Limited
Orchard House, Broad Street, Tylers Green, Cuckfield, West Sussex, RH17 5DZ, UK Used by permission.

O BREATH OF LIFE

```
      D                              G
v1   O Breath of Life, come sweeping through us
v2   O Wind of God come bend us break us

      Bm                            A
     Revive Your church with life and power
     Till humbly we confess our need

      D                              G
     O Breath of Life come cleanse renew us
     Then in Your tenderness remake us

      Bm            A              D
     And fit Your church to meet this hour
     Revive, restore; for this we plead


      G                              D
v3   O Breath of love come breathe within us

      G                          Bm    A
     Renewing thought and will and heart

      D                          G
     Come love of Christ afresh to win us

      Bm            A            D
     Revive Your church in every part


      D                          G
v4   Revive us Lord is zeal abating

      Bm                           A
     While harvest fields are vast and white?

      D                          G
     Revive us Lord the world is waiting

      Bm            A              D
     Equip Your church to spread the light
```

CHORDS USED IN THIS SONG

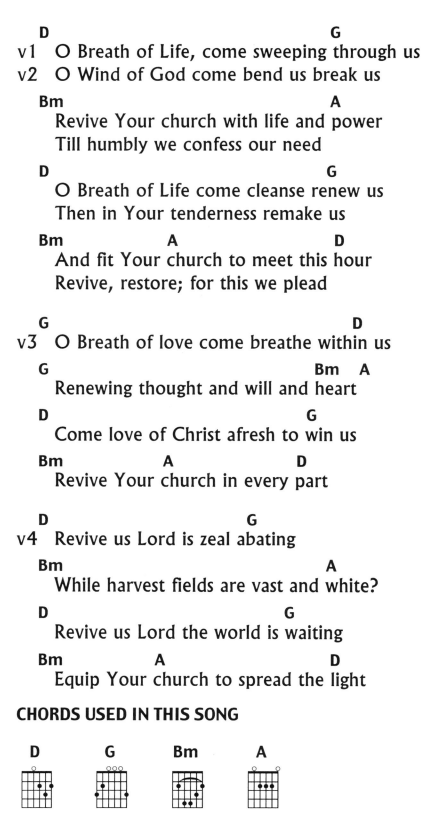

D   G   Bm   A

Words: Bessie Head (1850 - 1936))
Public Domain

Music: Andy Piercy
Copyright © 1999 IQ Music Limited
Orchard House, Broad Street, Tylers Green, Cuckfield, West Sussex, RH17 5DZ, UK Used by permission.

BE THE CENTRE

D
Jesus, be the centre

      A7sus4   **G/B**
Be my source, be my light

   D
Jesus

D
Jesus, be the centre

      A7sus4   **G/B**
Be my hope, be my song

   D
Jesus

        A7sus4   **D**
Be the fire in my heart

        A7sus4   **D**
Be the wind in these sails

        A7sus4   **D2/B**
Be the reason that I live

    A7sus4 G/B D
Jesus,   Jesus

D
Jesus, be my vision

      A7sus4   **G/B**
Be my path, be my guide

   D
Jesus

CHORDS USED IN THIS SONG

D   A7sus4   G/B   D2/B

Michael Frye
Copyright © 1999 Vineyard Songs (UK/Eire)
37 Blagdon Road, New Malden, KT3 4AH, England.
Used by permission.

MINE EYES HAVE SEEN THE GLORY

     A
Mine eyes have seen the glory of the coming of the Lord
     D   **A**
He is trampling out the vintage where the grapes of wrath are stored
                            C♯   **F♯m**
He has loosed the fateful lightning of His terrible swift sword;
 Bm7   **Esus E**   **A**
His truth is marching on

                   D   **A**
Glory, glory Alleluia! Glory, glory Alleluia!
               C♯ **F♯m**   **Bm7**   **Esus E**   **A**
Glory, glory Allelu - ia! His truth is marching on

      A
He has sounded forth the trumpet that shall never call retreat
     D   **A**
He is sifting out the hearts of men before His judgement seat
                          C♯   **F♯m**
O be swift my soul to answer Him be jubilant my feet!
 Bm7   **Esus E**   **A**
Our God is marching on

      A
In the beauty of the lilies Christ was born across the sea
     D   **A**
With a glory in His body that transfigures you and me
                          C♯   **F♯m**
Jesus died to make us holy now He lives to set us free
 Bm7   **Esus E**   **A**
His truth is marching on

CHORDS USED IN THIS SONG

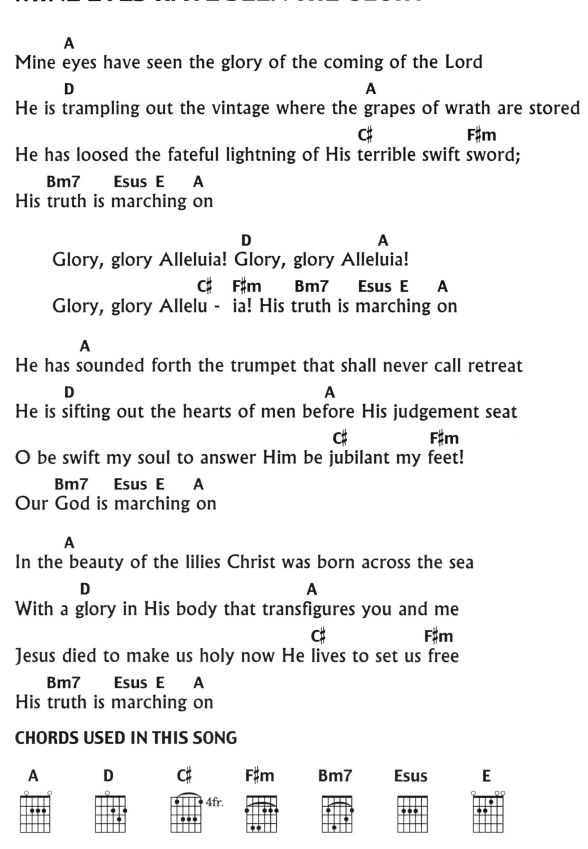

Julia W. Howe (1819-1910)

This arrangement by David Clifton © 1999 IQ Music Limited
Orchard House, Broad Street, Tylers Green, Cuckfield, West Sussex, RH17 5DZ, UK. Used by permission.

OPEN THE EYES OF MY HEART

E
Open the eyes of my heart Lord
B/D#
Open the eyes of my heart
       A/C#
I want to see You
       E
I want to see You
(Repeat)

          B   C#m
To see You high and lifted up
A2   B
Shining in the light of Your glory
                    C#m
Pour out Your power and love
          C#m   B
As we sing holy, holy, holy

E
Holy, holy, holy,
B/D#
Holy, holy, holy,
A/C#   A
Holy, holy, holy,
       E
I want to see You.

CHORDS USED IN THIS SONG

E   B/D#   A/C#   A   B   C#m   A2   F#m

Paul Baloche
Copyright © 1997 Integrity's Hosanna! Music/Kingsway's Thankyou Music
P.O. Box 75, Eastbourne, East Sussex, BN23 6NW, UK
Used by permission.

SALVATION BELONGS TO OUR GOD

```
     G          D/F♯        Em   Em/D
Salvation belongs to our God
        C    G/B   Am      D
Who sits upon the throne
G        D/F♯      Em   Em/D
And unto the Lamb
   C          G      C        G
Praise and glory, wisdom and thanks
   F          C         Dsus    D
Honour and power and strength


      G         D        C       Dsus D
   Be to our God for ever and ev - er
      G         D        C       Dsus D
   Be to our God for ever and ev - er
      G         D        C       Dsus D
   Be to our God for ever and ev - er!
      G
   Amen!


      G          D/F♯           Em   Em/D
   And we the redeemed shall be strong
      C  G/B       Am   D
   In purpose and uni- ty,
G    D/F♯      Em   Em/D
Declaring aloud
   C          G      C        G
Praise and glory, wisdom and thanks
   F          C         Dsus    D
Honour and power and strength
```

CHORDS USED IN THIS SONG

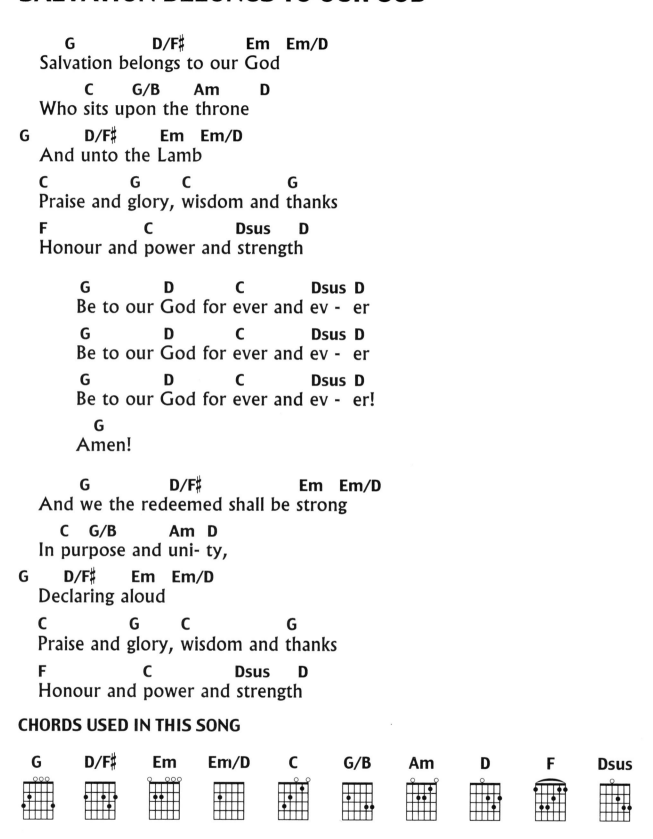

G   D/F♯   Em   Em/D   C   G/B   Am   D   F   Dsus

Adrian Turner and Pat Turner
Copyright © 1985 Restoration Music Ltd. Administered by CopyCare
P.O. Box 77, Hailsham, East Sussex, BN27 3EF, UK
Used by permission.

O LORD HEAR MY PRAYER

Em   Em7
O Lord hear my prayer,

C6   D7sus4
O Lord hear my prayer:

G/B   C   Am6   Bsus4 B
When I call, answer me.

Em   Em7
O Lord hear my prayer,

C6   D7sus4
O Lord hear my prayer.

Em   Am B   Em
Come and listen to me.

CHORDS USED IN THIS SONG

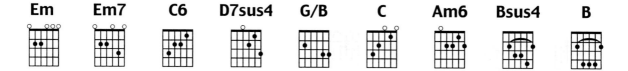

Em   Em7   C6   D7sus4   G/B   C   Am6   Bsus4   B

Jacques Berthier
Copyright © 1984 Ateliers et Presses de Taizé
Taizé-Communauté, F-71250, France.
Used by permission.

IF I RISE

```
Em                   C
   If I rise on the wings of the dawn
Em                       C
   If I rest on the far side of the sea
D                        C
   Even there Your arms will keep me warm
D                        C
   Even there Your loving hand is sure to guide me

Em                       C
   From Your Spirit where can I go?
Em                           C
   From Your presence where can I flee?
D                            C
   You are there in the ocean far below
D                        C
   I go up to the heavens You are there beside me

G                               D
   You have searched and You see
         Am            C
   All of me, all of me
G                       D
   I will give willingly
         Am            C        (Em)
   All of me, all of me
```

CHORDS USED IN THIS SONG

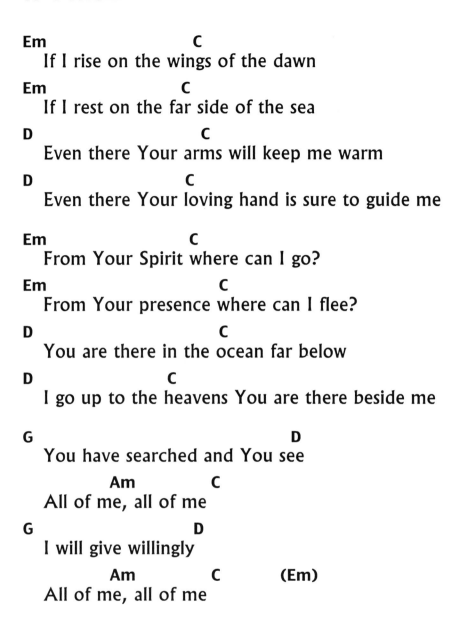

Em   C   D   G   Am

Jamie Haith
Copyright © 1997 IQ Music Limited
Orchard House, Broad Street, Tylers Green, Cuckfield, West Sussex, RH17 5DZ, UK
Used by permission.

BREATHE

A2   D2/A
This is the air I breathe

A2   D2/A
This is the air I breathe

A2   E/G♯ F♯m   E D2 F♯m   E
Your holy presence   living   in me

A2   D2/A
This is my daily bread

A2   D2/A
This is my daily bread

A2   E/G♯ F♯m E D2   F♯m   E
Your very word   spoken   to me

          A E/G♯ F♯m E   D2   F♯m   E
And I,   I'm desperate for You

          A E/G♯ F♯m E   D2   F♯m   E
And I,   I'm desperate for You

CHORDS USED IN THIS SONG

A2   D2/A   E/G♯   F♯m   E   D2

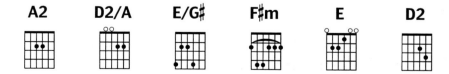

Marie Barnet

We come to you with a heart of thanks for Your love

To be a living sacrifice, brought with love

We come to You with a heart of thanks for Your love

An offering of all we are, brought with love

All creation looks to You

All provision, comes from You

In every sunrise, hope shines through

For Your mercy, we thank You

We come to You with a song of praise for Your love

The music of our soul's delight brought with love

We come to You with a song of praise for Your love

Sounds of joy and gratefulness brought with love

All creation looks to You

All provision comes from You

In every rhythm we thank You, for Your love

(In every season we thank You, for Your love.)

Brian Doerksen & Steve Mitchinson
Copyright © 1999 Vineyard Songs (UK/Eire)
37 Blagdon Road, New Malden, KT3 4AH, England.
Used by permission.

Lift up your heads, O you gates

Swing wide you everlasting doors

Lift up your heads, O you gates

Swing wide you everlasting doors

That the King of Glory may come in

That the King of Glory may come in

That the King of Glory may come in

That the King of Glory may come in

Up from the dead He ascends

Through every rank of heavenly power

Let heaven prepare the highest place

Throw wide the everlasting doors

With trumpet blast and shouts of joy

All heaven greets the risen King

With angel choirs, come line the way

Throw wide the gates and welcome Him

Who is like our God?

Who is like our God?

Holy and intimate, tender and strong,

Patient and powerful,

Who is like our God?

Who is like our God?

Who is like our God?

Mighty and innocent, jealous and kind,

Sovereign and merciful,

Who is like our God?

All of man's glory fades away

Like a spring flower in the rain.

No fallen angel is worthy to be worshipped,

Nor anything created.

Who is like our God?

Who is like our God?

Brian Duane, Brian Doerksen & Brian Thiessen
Copyright © 1995 Vineyard Songs (UK/Eire)
37 Blagdon Road, New Malden, KT3 4AH, England.
Used by permission.

1. Take my life and let it be
   Consecrated Lord to Thee
   Take my moments and my days
   Let them flow in ceaseless praise

2. Take my hands and let them move
   At the impulse of Thy love
   Take my feet and let them be
   Swift and beautiful for Thee

3. Take my voice and let me sing
   Always only for my King
   Take my lips and let them be
   Filled with messages from Thee

Words: Frances R Havergal (1874)
Public Domain

Music: David Clifton/Phil Baggaley
Copyright © 1998 IQ Music Limited
Orchard House, Broad Street, Tylers Green, Cuckfield, West Sussex, RH17 5DZ, UK
Used by permission.

4. Take my silver and my gold
   Not a mite would I withhold
   Take my intellect and use
   Every power as Thou shalt choose

5. Take my will and make it Thine
   It shall be no longer mine
   Take my heart it is Thine own
   It shall be Thy royal throne

6. Take my love my Lord I pour
   At Thy feet its treasure store
   Take myself and I will be
   Ever only all for Thee

Words: Frances R Havergal (1874)
Public Domain

Music: David Clifton/Phil Baggaley
Copyright © 1998 IQ Music Limited
Orchard House, Broad Street, Tylers Green, Cuckfield, West Sussex, RH17 5DZ, UK
Used by permission.

O Breath of Life, come sweeping through us

Revive Your church with life and power

O Breath of Life come cleanse renew us

And fit Your church to meet this hour

O Wind of God come bend us break us

Till humbly we confess our need

Then in Your tenderness remake us

Revive, restore; for this we plead

O Breath of love come breathe within us

Renewing thought and will and heart

Come love of Christ afresh to win us

Revive Your church in every part

Revive us Lord is zeal abating

While harvest fields are vast and white?

Revive us Lord the world is waiting

Equip Your church to spread the light

Words: Bessie Head (1850 - 1936)
Public Domain

Music: Andy Piercy
Copyright © 1999 IQ Music Limited
Orchard House, Broad Street, Tylers Green, Cuckfield, West Sussex, RH17 5DZ, UK
Used by permission.

Jesus, be the centre
Be my source, be my light
Jesus

Jesus, be the centre
Be my hope, be my song
Jesus

    Be the fire in my heart
    Be the wind in these sails
    Be the reason that I live
    Jesus, Jesus

Jesus, be my vision
Be my path, be my guide
Jesus

Mine eyes have seen the glory

Of the coming of the Lord

He is trampling out the vintage

Where the grapes of wrath are stored

He has loosed the fateful lightning

Of His terrible swift sword;

His truth is marching on

Glory, glory Alleluia!

Glory, glory Alleluia!

Glory, glory Alleluia!

His truth is marching on

He has sounded forth the trumpet

That shall never call retreat

He is sifting out the hearts of men

Before His judgement seat

O be swift my soul to answer Him

Be jubilant my feet! Our God is marching on

Julia W. Howe (1819-1910)
This arrangement by David Clifton © 1999 IQ Music Limited
Orchard House, Broad Street, Tylers Green, Cuckfield, West Sussex, RH17 5DZ, UK
Used by permission.

In the beauty of the lilies

Christ was born across the sea

With a glory in His body

That transfigures you and me

Jesus died to make us holy

Now He lives to set us free

His truth is marching on

Glory, glory Alleluia!

Glory, glory Alleluia!

Glory, glory Alleluia!

His truth is marching on

Julia W. Howe (1819-1910)
This arrangement by David Clifton. Copyright © 1999 IQ Music Limited
Orchard House, Broad Street, Tylers Green, Cuckfield, West Sussex, RH17 5DZ, UK
Used by permission.

Open the eyes of my heart Lord

Open the eyes of my heart

I want to see You

I want to see You

To see You high and lifted up

Shining in the light of Your glory

Pour out Your power and love

As we sing holy, holy, holy

Holy, holy, holy,

Holy, holy, holy,

Holy, holy, holy,

I want to see You.

Paul Baloche
Copyright © 1997 Integrity's Hosanna Music/Kingsway's Thankyou Music
P.O. Box 75, Eastbourne, East Sussex, BN23 6NW, UK
Used by permission.

Salvation belongs to our God

Who sits upon the throne

And unto the Lamb

Praise and glory

Wisdom and thanks

Honour and power and strength

> Be to our God for ever and ever
> Be to our God for ever and ever
> Be to our God for ever and ever!
> Amen!

And we the redeemed shall be strong

In purpose and unity, declaring aloud

Praise and glory, wisdom and thanks

Honour and power and strength

Adrian Turner and Pat Turner
Copyright © 1985 Restoration Music Ltd. Administered by CopyCare
P.O. Box 77, Hailsham, East Sussex, BN27 3EF, UK
Used by permission.

O Lord hear my prayer,

O Lord hear my prayer:

When I call, answer me.

O Lord hear my prayer,

O Lord hear my prayer.

Come and listen to me.

Jacques Berthier
Copyright © 1984 Ateliers et Presses de Taizé
Taizé-Communauté, F-71250, France.
Used by permission.

If I rise on the wings of the dawn

If I rest on the far side of the sea

Even there Your arms will keep me warm

Even there Your loving hand is sure to guide me

From Your Spirit where can I go?

From Your presence where can I flee?

You are there in the ocean far below

I go up to the heavens You are there beside me

You have searched and You see

All of me, all of me

I will give willingly

All of me, all of me

Jamie Haith
Copyright © 1997 IQ Music Limited
Orchard House, Broad Street, Tylers Green, Cuckfield, West Sussex, RH17 5DZ, UK
Used by permission.

This is the air I breathe

This is the air I breathe

Your holy presence living in me

This is my daily bread

This is my daily bread

Your very word spoken to me

And I, I'm desperate for you

And I, I'm lost without you

Marie Barnet
Copyright © 1995 Mercy/Vineyard Publishing/Music Services. Administered by CopyCare
P.O. Box 77, Hailsham, East Sussex, BN27 3EF, UK.
Used by permission.